Secrets Of
Auto Financing

Non-Prime Auto Financing and What
You Should Know Before You Buy

copyright©2008
G. L. Evans

We've all heard it. Good credit, bad credit, no credit… no problem. Divorce, bankruptcy, repossession. Re-establish your credit… we finance anyone.

What does it all mean? How does it work? What kind of car can I buy? How much down payment do I need? Will I get ripped off?

This book will answer these questions, and more, in an easy to understand, simple format.

Table of Contents

Appendices

4

Chapter 1:

<u>What Is Non-Prime Financing?</u>

Non-prime financing is a catch-all term for a number of different lending programs, all of which are designed to finance cars for people who cannot obtain a loan from a standard financial institution. Examples of standard (or prime) financial institutions include banks, credit unions and manufacturer's finance companies like GMAC, Ford Motor Credit, etc.

Other terms for non-prime financing include sub-prime, secondary financing, second chance financing, buy-here pay-here and in-house financing. Whatever it is called, they all try to accomplish the same thing: loaning money for cars to people with difficulty financing with prime lenders.

The first thing to understand about non-prime financing is that it is not cheap. You will undoubtedly pay a price for the risk taken by the lender. The typical repossession rate for a non-prime lender is between 20%

and 30%. Most of these result in considerable loss. As a result, in order to turn an overall profit, the lender must charge high fees and interest rates. Think of it as the SR-22 insurance of the credit world.

The good news is that you can re-establish your credit and qualify for better terms on your next car loan if you make your car payment, and any other payments you have, on time.

That being said, you still don't have to break your budget to drive a car. If you approach your purchase with reasonable expectations of what you can afford and are willing to drive, you can bring home a reliable vehicle, at an affordable payment, for a responsible loan term.

Chapter 2:

Types of Non-Prime Financing

While there are a myriad of companies offering non-prime financing, we can group them all into three basic categories. Following is a brief description of each.

1. Customer-direct finance companies.

These are companies that have no affiliation in any way with the dealer. You can find these in storefronts of strip malls or on the internet. They lend money directly to the customer to purchase a car. This is the most difficult, but also the most cost effective means, to obtain non-prime financing. By arranging financing through one of them before shopping for a car, you can negotiate a better cash price on your purchase. A previous relationship with the company and/or more marginal credit is usually helpful. Try this first, but don't be discouraged if you are turned down.

One other benefit of using one of these companies is that they normally will report to the credit bureau(s).

2. Point-of-sale finance companies.

These are companies with whom dealers have an agreement to finance their customers. Because of this relationship, the dealer knows what criteria these companies use to approve loans. Armed with all your information, the dealer can match your profile to the company with the best program for you.

The biggest catch with this type of company is that you will pay a premium price for the car. Dealers do not typically discount cars sold under these programs because the finance company keeps a reserve amount of the total amount financed in order to defray the risk involved. This results in the dealer receiving less than the sale price of the car.

The advantage of using this over in-house dealer financing is that you can purchase a newer car with less down payment. The term is typically longer as well, keeping your monthly payment at a comfortable amount. These companies also will normally report to the credit bureau(s).

3. In-house or buy-here pay-here financing.

This type of financing is typical of smaller used car lots, as well as a few larger multi-location used car dealers. These loans are usually maintained by the original dealer and payments are made directly to them. Occasionally the loan is sold by the dealer to any of several other finance companies. If this occurs, the terms of the loan must remain the same according to law. This can be to your benefit, since the new finance company will commonly report to the credit bureau(s). Although some dealerships will report repossessions, most buy-here pay-here loans go unreported unless they are sold. If you do obtain one of these loans, the dealer will normally give you a credit reference upon request.

The down side to this type of financing is that you will typically have to settle for an older, higher mileage car.

Chapter 3:

Financing Criteria

The first step in determining your best finance option is to know what the lenders use as criteria to approve or deny loans. With few exceptions, these are pretty much standard. Following is a list of these criteria:

1. Prior credit history.

Let's face it, if it was any good you wouldn't be reading this book. The lenders know this, so don't let it stop you from applying.

2. Job time.

For most lenders this is very important. Being on the same job, or at least in the same field, for a length of time shows stability. One or two years is great. Three months is minimum for most of the more lenient lenders.

3. Residence time.

Again, this is important. If credit is not good, stability is what you need. Lenders want to know that you have a permanent residence where, if necessary, you can be found. Just like with job time, one to two years is preferable, or at least that much time in the area. Special circumstances, like moving for your job, can be considered as well.

4. Income.

This one should be obvious. Saying you can afford it and making the money to pay the payments can be two very different things. Lenders don't want you to overextend, and will therefore limit your monthly payment based on your gross income. This will, in turn, limit what car you are able to purchase. This is why you must be reasonable about what car you are willing to drive. Remember, when giving income on an application, give your gross income before any taxes or insurances are deducted.

Most lenders have minimum income requirements, usually starting about $1300-$1500 per month for individual applicants, $2500 or so per month for joint applications. This can vary widely depending on the lender.

5. Debt ratio.

This goes hand in hand with income. Debt ratio is simply the amount you pay out in bills each month, divided by your income. The higher the resulting number, the less likely you are to be approved for a loan. Things like high rent, other car loans, credit cards with balances, etc. will result in a high debt ratio. A good cosigner can sometimes be helpful if you are in this situation. Obviously, the less you have to pay each month, and the higher your income, the better your debt ratio will be. Lenders typically look for a debt ratio of 40% (.40) or less, including your new payment. If yours is over 50% (.50), start trying to pay off debt and/or look for a cosigner.

See Appendix A (pg. 25) for the formula to determine your own debt ratio.

6. Down payment.

We're talking about <u>buying</u> a car, not renting one. Buying requires an investment. The more you put down, the more likely the lender is to believe you won't quit paying, because you have more to lose if you do. While there are some buy-here pay-here dealers that will take as little as $500 down, you get what you pay for. If you want a decent car, try to come up with at least $1500-$2000 down. If you have less, your choices are more limited.

Chapter 4:

Proof and Verification

Non-prime finance lenders are very thorough when verifying information. They require proof that what is on your application is correct. You will need to provide documentation showing your income, as well as proof of your residence. Calls and/or faxes will be made to employers and landlords to verify that the information you have given is accurate. It is a good idea, if you can, to forewarn them that they will be contacted.

You will also be required to provide references, usually five or six, including names, addresses and phone numbers of friends and family.

Proof of physical damage insurance is a requirement on almost any car loan. This means that you must have collision and comprehensive, as well as liability insurance. Most people refer to this as full coverage. It is best to set this up with your insurance agent before you shop, so that you can call and get an insurance binder faxed to the dealer at the time of purchase. Be sure to give the agent the lender's name and address, as lienholder information, when you call for the binder. Insurance deductibles over $500 are generally not accepted by non-prime lenders. It is also in your own best interest to stay at $500 or less.

Now let's talk about what documentation you need. It is very important to provide your proof in a form that is acceptable to lenders. The following list shows what is and is not accepted as proof by most lenders.

Proof of income:

1. Computerized pay stub or pay information sheet showing year-to-date earnings and deductions.
   This is the best form of income proof that you can have. It is accepted by all lenders.

2. Handwritten company checks.

These are considered on a case-by-case basis. If your employer pays you using checks without computerized stubs, you will need copies of the front and back of the cancelled checks after they are returned by the bank to your employer. Usually the two most recent months are required.

3. Bank statements showing direct deposit of your pay.
This is another form of proof of income accepted by most lenders.

4. Bank statements showing your own deposits.
These will generally be accepted by lenders, provided they show regular deposits that verify the amount claimed as income on your application. Lenders will accept these on a case-by-case basis. If you must use these for your proof of income, be sure that you deposit all your income regularly and do not overdraw your account during the three months prior to your purchase. This is essential if you get paid by cash, handwritten checks or tips.

5. Tax returns, W-2's, 1099's.

These can be helpful, particularly at the beginning of the year when they are current. Lenders will often want them accompanied by bank statements and/or verification by an employer. If you are a subcontractor or self employed, this could be your best approach.

6. Letter from an employer.

This should be used as a last resort and is usually only accepted by smaller buy-here pay-here dealers, unless accompanied by bank statements showing deposits. If this is all you can provide, be sure to let the dealer know up front and be ready to settle for less car.

7. Income other than employment.

It is important to be able to prove all income claimed on your application. Be prepared to provide documentation showing retirement, social security, disability, annuity, trust or other income you may have.

Proof of residence:

1. Mortgage statement.
    If you are a homeowner, this the best documentation for proof of residence. A copy of your most recent statement should be satisfactory. If your mortgage is past due, you will most likely need to use a buy-here pay-here dealer.

2. Lease or lease-purchase agreement.
    If you are leasing a house or apartment, or are lease-purchasing a house or condo, a copy of the agreement, in your name, is the best proof you can provide. If you have roommate(s) on the lease with you, this will also show that the rent is shared and lower your debt ratio.

3. Utility bill.
    If you are not on a lease or mortgage, you should provide a bill in your name which is mailed to your residence address. Power, gas, phone or water bills are preferred.

4. Other mail.

If you have no bills in your name, you should provide something else that comes in the mail to you at your residence address. Bank statements can sometimes be used. Whatever you have will be considered on a case-by-case basis by the lender. Without proper proof of residence, you may have to rely on a buy-here pay-here loan.

5. Letter from landlord.

If you have nothing else, you can try a letter from your landlord or tenant where you reside. This is very flimsy proof of residence and most lenders will not accept it. Make the effort to get some kind of bill in your name and have it mailed to your address.

Chapter 5:

Get Prepared

Now you know the types of non- prime financing available, the criteria the lenders use to determine eligibility, and the documentation required to prove you meet the criteria. The next step is to gather what you will need when you apply. Start by getting together your proof of income and proof of residence. Then make a list of references on a separate sheet of paper with your name at the top. Remember, you will need 5 or 6 including name, address and phone number. You should make 2 or 3 copies of all of these to give to the dealer(s) from whom you want to buy your car. Also, shop insurance so you know who to call when you buy your car.

HOLD ON!!!

Now that you have everything together, take a good look at how accurate your documentation really is. Do you think it will help you qualify for a loan? Is your income accurately reflected in the documentation you have, or would you be able to provide better information if you wait for your next pay stub? Perhaps you should open a bank account and make sufficient deposits for 2-3 months in order to better prove your income.

Look at your proof of residence. Does it serve to show that you do indeed reside where you say? If not, try to get some kind of bill sent to the address in your name. Phone, gas, electric or water bills are the best. If you can't do this, get a cell phone in your name at your address or, again, a bank statement. Taking time and effort to have better documentation will help tremendously in the long run.

Remember these key things:

-Better proof
-Bigger down payment
-Lower debt ratio

These combined add up to a nicer car at better finance terms.

Now you have the information you need to make financing a car through a non- prime finance company smoother and easier. Use the following charts for quick reference in determining the type(s) that is best for your situation, and to get your credit on track.

Good Luck.

<u>Notes</u>

Appendix A:

Determining Your Debt Ratio

Your debt ratio is calculated by using the mathematical formula:

$$\frac{\text{expenses per month}}{\text{gross income per month}} = \text{debt ratio}$$

For example:
Joe has rent, a student loan and a credit card payment that total $700.00 per month. His new car payment will be $400.00 per month. Now his expenses will total $1100.00 per month. His gross income before any deductions is $2500.00 per month. His debt ratio is 44%, calculated as follows:

$$\frac{1100}{2500} = .44 \quad \text{or} \quad 44\%$$

Appendix B

<u>Summary Chart</u>

	Fair	Good	Better	Best
Proof of Income	Tax documents, Letter from employer	Bank statements showing deposits you have made yourself	Bank statements Showing direct deposit, copies of employer's canceled checks	Computer generated pay stubs
Proof of Residence	Letter from landlord	Other mail in your name	Utility bill in your name	Mortgage statement, lease in your name
Job Time	Less than 3 months	4 months-1 year	1-2 years	2 years or more
Residence Time	Less than 3 months	4 months-1 year	1-2 years	2 years or more
Debt Ratio	Over 50%	45-50%	40-45%	Under 40%

Appendix C

<u>Reference List</u>

	Name	Address	Phone#
1			
2			
3			
4			
5			
6			

Notes